THE MINISTER'S CAT

An A-Z of CATS in VERSE

THE MINISTER'S CAT

An A-Z of CATS in VERSE

by

DOUGLAS KYNOCH

Illustrated by
NORMAN GLEN

SCOTTISH CULTURAL PRESS

First published 1994
Scottish Cultural Press
PO Box 106
Aberdeen AB9 8ZE
Tel/Fax: 01224 583777

British Library Cataloguing in Publication Data
A catalogue record for this book is available
from the British Library

ISBN: 1 898218 18 8

Printed by
Bell & Bain, Glasgow

Dedicated to
'the whole nation of cattes'
and in memory of six in particular!

ACKNOWLEDGEMENTS

The author thanks Gladys Menhinick for reading the manuscript and offering encouragement.

The illustrator wishes to record his indebtedness to his models: Custer, Chivers, Willow, Maclean, Casey and Connie.

The illustration showing 'Melchizedek, the musical cat' is based on the concept of the HIS MASTER'S VOICE Trade Mark and is produced with the kind permission of the Trade Mark owner.

INTRODUCTION

A parlour game of great popularity at one time, especially in Scotland, 'The Minister's Cat' is still played today here and there. The object of the game is to find unusual words to describe the cat belonging to the church minister. In the first round, each member of the company takes it in turn to think of an adjective beginning with the letter 'A'. The first player may decide that "the minister's cat is an *authoritarian* cat", the second player that it is "an *anti-social* cat". In the second round, descriptive words are required beginning with 'B'; and so on through the alphabet.

The cats described here were born of imagination. Any resemblance to domestic pets living or dead is purely coincidental. It seemed fitting that clergy cats should bear names drawn from the Bible. There being no biblical names with the initial letters W, X and Y, certain disgraceful devices had to be resorted to. Enough z.

CONTENTS

. . . AN AMBITIOUS CAT

Abraham's certain as certain can be
That one day, he'll climb to the top of the tree.
Oozing with talent, he's got what it takes;
And all that he needs are a few lucky breaks.
Given good luck and some startling PR,
There's nothing to stop him becoming a star,
Followed around by the popular press,
Intent on reporting his latest success.

He pictures his triumphs with tightly shut eyes:
His Booker Award and his Pulitzer Prize;
The keys of the city, a portrait in oils;
A knighthood, an Oscar, a luncheon at Foyle's;
The Order of Merit, the Croix de Lorraine;
The Wimbledon trophy filled up with champagne;
And lastly, to crown a triumphant career,
He's voted by vets "Best Dressed Cat of the Year."

Abraham's certain as certain can be
That one day, he'll climb to the top of the tree.
Now, merely dreaming his dreams of renown,
He's purring like mad on a branch farther down.

. . . A BENEVOLENT CAT

Dear Bathsheba*, since kittenhood,
Has spent her life in doing good.
Brought up to see all cats as brothers,
Her first concern has been for others;
And mainly, those of low degree,
Who are less fortunate than she.
For such, at very little warning,
She'll organise a coffee morning.
At other times, she'll put her all
Into a cake and candy stall,
A jumble sale or sponsored walking.
She's doing, while the rest are talking.
She volunteers her willing paws
To every charitable cause:
To Sunday schools and Foreign Missions;
Blind dogs and indigent musicians;
To orphaned mice and wayward rats;
Impoverished old gentlecats;
A fund for renovating abbeys;
The welfare of unmarried tabbies
(On whose behalf, she's shortly due
To start a Nearly Mew shop too).
She keeps used stamps and saves up coppers;
She follows silver paper droppers;
She scours the streets and rubbish bins
For aluminium rings from tins;
And always with the self-same goal:
To raise some cash "for some poor soul".
A grateful world (which this one ain't!)
Would make dear Bathsheba a saint.

* (The rhythm should at once suggest
Which syllable should here be stressed.)

. . . A CANNY CAT

The moment you meet him, it's perfectly plain:
There's no cat alive who's as canny as Cain.
His boots are unsightly and through at the soles;
His hanky's like netting, less hanky than holes.
He knows if it's used that it's certain to rip,
So frequently settles instead for a drip.
He carries a brolly for fear of a soak;
But keeps it rolled up, lest he damage a spoke.
In days that are not so long gone as you think,
He'd fill his pen daily with Post Office ink.
As far as those manacled ballpoints allow,
He answers his mail in the post office now!
It must be so hard for his wife and his kittens;
They say that she brings them all up on a pittance.
He takes them out visiting night after night,
To save on the outlay for heating and light;
And hopes, when they've watched her TV for a spell,
Their hostess will offer them supper as well.
You'd think he was destitute, broke, on the rocks;
And yet, he has hundreds of thousands in stocks.
He's eager, it seems, to out-thrift Aberdeen.
I said he was canny - he's dreadfully mean!

. . . A DEEP CAT

Delilah's expression is fixed as the Sphinx;
She stares at you quite without blinking.
She shows that detachment observed among shrinks:
You never know what she is thinking.

Emotions are things that she closely controls;
She seems to disdain the dramatic.
While others are busily baring their souls,
She opts to remain enigmatic.

Opinions, she plainly prefers to eschew,
As if she believed them "unsuitable".
If ever you try to solicit her view,
You'll find her, as always, inscrutable.

She's quite the most difficult cat to impress;
Yes, even with something spectacular.
It's slightly dismaying, I have to confess,
When someone's so blandly oracular.

A cynic once said that she's really asleep,
Eyes open, to keep her from snoring.
Her circle will tell you Delilah is "deep".
I wonder. Perhaps she's just boring!

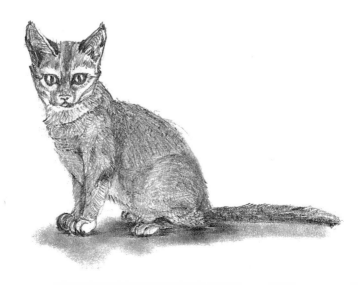

. . . AN ELUSIVE CAT

Crikey! Where's Enoch? It's twenty past eight!
I *said* we should leave him at home. We'll be late!
Just let me catch him, I'll wring his sweet neck.
The taxi will be at the door in a sec.
Standing there gawping won't help. Use your heads!
Go round all the curtains, look under the beds!
Try in the cubby-hole under the stair!
No, not in his basket. He's *never* in there!
See if he's messing with George's meccano!
Or being Houdini behind the piano!
Check all the cupboards and drawers - and the bin!
The poor little blighter, he might be shut in!
Comb the whole house for a pitiful cry!
You can't hear a dicky bird? Neither can I.
Why this darned suitcase won't fasten beats me!
Let's rattle his dish and he'll think it's his tea!
Give us a hand with this case; I'm all thumbs!
I'll strangle that cat, when he finally comes.
D'you hear what I hear? A faint little mew?
No wonder this bag won't shut. Enoch, it's YOU!

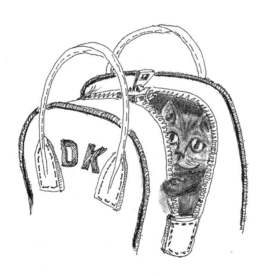

. . . A FREAKY CAT

Never a cat you would think of as striking,
Felix is now quite a sight to be seen.
Whether or not it's to anyone's liking,
Felix's fur has been dyed apple-green.

As for his lady-friend, hers is bright scarlet.
People must think they've gone clean round the bend:
Him like a circus clown, her like a harlot.
Where in the world is it going to end?

Felix was once such a steady young tomcat,
Good at his lessons and kind to his mum.
She would prefer a discreet ban-the-bomb cat
To one with a safety-pin stuck through his tum.

Now, in his ear, there's a single gold earring.
Is it poetic? Or merely perverse?
Do have a care what you say in his hearing.
If you provoke him, he'll do something worse!

Why is he never without a transistor?
Why must he plonk that electric guitar?
Why does he varnish his nails like his sister?
Why must he be so devoutly bizarre?

. . . A GUILTY CAT

Gomer has washed her paws again.
Is there no end to the licking?
Barely a moment of rest; and then,
She returns to her ritual slicking.

So it goes on by night and day.
Something must surely compel her.
Gomer is washing her life away.
Why on earth doesn't someone tell her?

All this ablution's of no avail;
Nothing can satisfy Gomer.
Personal hygiene on such a scale
Is, in fact, a complete misnomer.

Cleansing away an imagined spot
Now has become an obsession.
Is there a name for what she's got?
Paranoia? Acute depression?

Lady Macbeth was much the same
After the murder of Duncan.
Everything's pointing at who's to blame
For the death of that poor shubunkin.

. . . A HOMESICK CAT

Born on a far-away westerly island
Swept by a stormy south-easterly gale,
Old Hezekiah's essentially Highland,
Right from his ears to the tip of his tail.

Ask him to talk about home and he'll wail you
One of the sorrowful songs of the West.
"Heederum, hiderum, ho" will assail you,
Gaelic mouse music is what he sings best.

Gaelic is all that he spoke till eleven,
Picking it up at his grandmother's knee.
Fancy employing 'the language of heaven'
To tell Hezekiah to come for his tea!

Poor Hezekiah, morose on the mainland,
Loathing the bedlam-let-loose on the streets,
Longs in his heart to escape this insane land,
Pack it all in and return to his peats.

What he loves most is an island reunion:
Yarning and yearning and taking a skite*.
Hezzie's teetotal except for communion,
Weddings, interments and Saturday night.

* *a drink*

. . . AN INQUISITIVE CAT

Isaiah showed signs from his earliest youth
Of being a serious seeker of truth;
And every new day, his acquaintanceship found him
Exploring the world and the wonders around him.
No cranny or crook was left open to doubt;
There wasn't a corner he didn't suss out.
He'd venture a paw and he seldom withdrew it;
If anyone opened a door, he walked through it.
What all this denoted was clear to discern:
A hunger and thirsting for new things to learn.
He's started to read, with fanatical fervour:
And loves to tear into *The Times* and *Observer*.
On other occasions, you'll happen to look
And catch him consulting a reference book.
(Thereafter, his conduct is not to his credit:
He nibbles the covers to show that he's read it!)
Your letters, no matter how often you gripe,
He's pleased to peruse upside-down as you type.
You'd cover them up, could you only contrive it;
There *are* certain things that you like to keep private.
You'd tell him to mind his own business and go;
Yet it's not that he's nosey; just DESP'RATE TO KNOW.

. . . A JEALOUS CAT

Joanna cared neither for dog nor cat;
Not for bird nor for mole nor mouse;
But, at every turn, her first concern
Was her master, the man of the house.

She'd follow behind him from room to room;
She would lie on his lap at night.
As he stroked her fur, she'd purr and purr
A delirious song of delight.

The birth of her kitten was almost due,
When she'd gone to his door at first.
What he'd taken in, distressed and thin,
Was a waif who'd known hunger and thirst.

Devotion took root in a grateful heart,
Blooming still, when the kitten came;
For maternal care left love to spare;
And affection for him was the same.

The kitten's deciding to love him too
Caused Joanna acute dismay.
A resentment stirred; she seldom purred;
And she yowled, when she caught them at play.

The want of exclusiveness pained her so:
Having part, who had once the whole.
And her cries gave vent to lost content,
As her anguish disfigured her soul.

The torment redoubled with every dawn;
But the pain, though intense, was brief;
For a wayward star and a passing car
Put an end to her life and her grief.

Joanna was mourned by the man she left.
Though her dying was hard to bear,
He would sometimes say, things were best that way:
It had not been her nature to share.

. . . A KLEPTOMANIAC CAT

Kish was an unrepentant fiddler,
Scarcely ever statuesque!
Oh, what a trifler! What a twiddler!
Mostly on the writing desk!

Spectacles, scissors, rulers, stencils,
Everything became his toy.
Mad about ball-point pens and pencils!
How the habit did annoy!

Soon he began to take away things;
But his memory was slack.
Once he had wearied of his playthings,
He forgot to bring them back.

Dyed in the wool, the weakness lingered,
Till a nightmare did the trick.
Kish, in the dream, was caught light-fingered;
And he landed up in nick.

Brought to a courtroom quite astonished,
Judges asked him "Where's your sense?"
Then, he was cautioned and admonished,
As it was his first offence.

This was sufficient retribution
(Talk about instantaneous cures!)
Kish was to make a resolution:
"Keep your paws off what's not yours!"

. . . A LANGUID CAT

Draped on a chair of padded dralon,
Lazily watching a game of chess,
All she would need is to put a veil on
To be an Arabian Nights princess.

Still as a sitter for a painter,
Barely averting her long, straight gaze;
Could there be anything cooler, quainter
In these rough-and-tumble and ragtag days?

No matter what goes on around her,
Lydia never appears to care.
Seems there is nothing can astound her
Or shake that absurdly complacent air.

Thoughts about work or earning livings
Never have entered her pretty head;
Nor has she even faint misgivings
That this is her life as it should be led.

Born of the lucky leisured classes,
Lydia lolls the whole day through,
Surer with every year that passes,
That this is the civilised thing to do.

. . . A MUSICAL CAT

Melchizedek wasn't obedient;
He'd never come in when you called.
He came, when he thought it expedient;
Or mischief eventually palled.

This most unattractive of attitudes
Is far from uncommon today;
And, deaf to admonit'ry platitudes,
Melchizedek went his own way.

One night, as his owner was calling him
And whistling a song to the moon,
The cat showed the sound was enthralling him;
And ran to the source of the tune.

At thoughts that the music enraptured him,
The owner felt tempted to scoff;
But quickly bent over and captured him,
Before the effect should wear off.

He promptly exploded in merriment
As soon as he got him indoors;
And, planning a simple experiment
With Melkie, got down on all fours.

His whistling of Sullivan choruses
Produced a response as before;
For, purring like two brontosauruses,
Melchizedek clearly cried "More!"

Ignoring these irrationalities,
And being extremely astute,
The owner saw great practicalities
In having an "Orpheus lute".

At meals, there's no cause now to remonstrate;
A whistle's as good as a gong,
Which seems very plainly to demonstrate
The power of the popular song.

. . . A NUCLEAR CAT

Noah is digging a whopping great hole.
He's not hunting treasure; he's not mining coal.
Holes form a part of his daily routine;
But this one's much bigger than they've ever been.
More of a burrow, in fact, than a hole,
It might suit a rabbit or even a mole,
Being quite deep and sufficiently wide
To let one take refuge in comfort inside.
Noah explains, if you ask what it's for,
He's dug it in case of a nuclear war.
This is his shelter. As simple as that.
For Noah is known as the nuclear cat.

Noah admits that he hadn't a clue.
A Government booklet described what to do.
This covered basic construction alone,
So all the refinements are strictly his own:
Curtains, for instance, made up from pink chintz;
The three flying ducks and the Tretchikoff prints.
Once he has finished his own maisonette,
He plans to start work on another, to let.
Banking on taking a fortnight at most,
He's got a large notice all ready to post:
"HIGHLY DESIRABLE UNDERGROUND FLAT!
FULL DETAILS FROM NOAH, THE NUCLEAR CAT!"

. . . AN OMNIPRESENT CAT

Obadiah's on the sofa;
Obadiah's on the chair.
No, he isn't there in person;
But they're covered in his hair.

Obadiah's on the carpet;
Obadiah's on the mat.
He's perpetually moulting,
That infuriating cat.

Obadiah's on my sweaters;
Obadiah's on my suit.
When I'm going out on business,
I could kill the little brute.

Obadiah's on the bedspread;
On the pillow as I sleep.
If he doesn't keep his hair on,
I shall shear him like a sheep.

I've been asking Obadiah,
As he grudges me his purr,
In the name of all that's feline,
Why he's prodigal with fur.

Obadiah, to his credit,
Has a reason for the hair:
He's afraid he'll be forgotten
Any time he isn't there.

It's a token of his presence,
When he's temporar'ly gone;
And a comforting assurance
That his mem'ry lingers on.

. . . A PACIFIST CAT

Pilate was always a peace-loving cat;
He flees at the sign of a crisis.
If ever, by chance, he encounters a rat,
It's left to its sordid devices.

True that he once trapped a petrified mouse
It seemed he might well do away with;
But why he manoeuvred it into the house
Was merely for someone to play with.

Not even birds are considered his foes;
The garden is full of young friskers.
They plunder the fruit bushes under his nose.
In time, they'll be tweaking his whiskers!

Spiders and flies are immune from attack;
They go their sweet way quite unharassed.
The flies buzz around him, when things get too slack.
The other cats cringe. They're embarrassed!

Hunting, says Pilate, is morally wrong;
His conscience forbids him to do it.
What piffle! He's had it too easy too long.
He's idle! There's nothing more to it!

. . .A QUIXOTIC CAT

Who's always at his most unruly
Attacking that ignoble bully,
The dangling rope on the kitchen pulley?
Quartus!

Who dashes fiercely to the fray,
When hostile forces block the way;
And leaves *The Guardian* in disarray?
Quartus!

Who rushes in with swift redress
To save a tabby in distress;
And makes the bedspread a tangled mess?
Quartus!

Who goes on monster-hunting treks?
Who seizes serpents by their necks;
And chews up all the electric flex?
Quartus!

And who, when strength begins to fail,
Curls up at last with folded tail
To dream a dream of the Holy Grail?
Why, Quartus!

. . . A REFINED CAT

It happened this morning that somebody said
"You can tell that Rebecca is very well bred".
When pressed, he revealed that her "breeding" consists
In just one little habit in which she persists:
Whenever she's having a meal, flesh or fish,
There's a piece that gets left at the side of the dish.
No matter how hungry, she thinks it polite
To eat all she is given except the last bite,
An idiosyncrasy some of us feel
To be more affectation than truly genteel.
And while I have no wish at all to be rude,
It is also uncommonly wasteful of food;
And, rather like coffee gone cold in the cup,
Is a terrible nuisance to those who clear up.
It's doubtful Rebecca will come to see sense;
The effect of the formative years is immense.
It may be impossible now *not* to do
What her well-meaning mother conditioned her to.
In any event, would re-training be kind,
When Rebecca believes that she's being refined?

. . . A SENSITIVE CAT

Never a cat to seek attention,
When there isn't any time;
Solomon's gift for apprehension
Is less feline than sublime.

Never a cat to drive you scatty
With an irritating mew,
Solomon can be very chatty;
But he can be silent too.

Never a mood that goes unheeded:
Always sensing what is what,
Solomon knows when he is needed
And he knows when he is not.

Never in league with those who brand you
An unfathomable man.
Solomon may not understand you;
But he acts as if he can.

Keeping in tune is fundamental
With a certain kind of cat.
Where is the human friend as gentle
Or as comforting as that?

. . . A TIMOROUS CAT

Tabitha, Tabitha, no need to scat!
A footstep is nothing to fear.
Come back to your dinner, ridiculous cat!
There's no one can harm you in here.

Tabitha's one of the timorous kind,
As nervous as – well, as a kitten.
She'd win any contest promoted to find
The jumpiest moggy in Britain.

Is it that something's affected the brain,
To render her this highly strung?
It's certainly not that her life is a strain.
Perhaps she was damaged when young.

Trauma at birth or an infantile shock
May account for her delicate state.
Perhaps some severe psychological knock
She's not come to terms with to date.

Tabitha starts at each sound that we make,
As if there were something amiss.
There must be a powder or pill she can take.
We can't go round creeping like this!

. . . AN UNORTHODOX CAT

There are attributes said to belong to a cat,
Behaviour we say is their wont;
Clear patterns of doing, like purring and mewing,
Which most other quadrupeds don't.

But Uzziah is far from an average cat;
He seldom adheres to the norms.
His characteristics defy all statistics;
There's little to which he conforms.

For example, he's never been partial to milk;
And cream just gets left in the dish.
Not even a sliver of lightly cooked liver
Will tempt him. And neither will fish!

It's a shame he dislikes dainty morsels like these,
When other cats find them so good.
What does make him purry is Indian curry,
With lemon meringue for a pud.

It's reported that cats won't go out in the rain;
They're wary of wetting their feet,
A rule which he muddles by splashing through puddles.
For him, its a positive treat.

The convention observed when you're stroking a cat
Is never to rub the wrong way.
Uzziah (no joking!) adores backward stroking.
He'd love if you did it all day.

Where the typical cat settles close to the fire,
Uzziah sits out in the hall.
So much odd-man-outing gives rise to ones doubting
He's really a cat after all!

. . . A VANISHING CAT

Who gave poor Vashti this liquid to drink?
It's some of the children's invisible ink.
Send for the vet! But he'll have to be quick.
She drank quite a lot and she's bound to be sick.
Look under 'V' in the telephone book;
Jack Vosper's his name and . . . Good gracious! Just look!
Maybe I'm wrong; but I'm sure as can be
That Vashti had *four* paws. Well, now she has three.
Merciful heavens! It's worse than I feared!
Most of her beautiful tail's disappeared.
Years of good feeding and this is our thanks!
Now we get left with a three-footed Manx!
Did I say three feet? That's no longer true.
She's just lost another; she's only got two.
Strange she shows no sign of missing them yet.
Perhaps she still sees them. Oh, where is that vet?
Only her head is left now and two feet.
Unless he comes soon, there'll be nothing to treat.
Now the two feet are away; and her ears!
Grab hold of her face before that disappears!
Beg her forgiveness for things that we've said!
And give her a kiss on what's left of her head!
Stay with us, Vashti! We need you! We do!
The vet's just arrived and . . . Whoops! Vashti, adieu!

. . . A WELL-INTENTIONED CAT

He meant not to claw at the carpet again;
But I'm sorry to say that he did it.
He just felt the urge; and, too late to refrain,
It happened before he gave thought.
He meant not to jump on the table at tea;
But he did it, the rascal. He did it.
He had just smelled a smell that he wanted to see
And forgot every rule he'd been taught.

Uri-Uriah, as everyone mentions,
You do have such thoroughly good intentions.

He meant not to trample the plants we'd put in;
But it pains me to tell you he's done it.
He knew it was reckoned a cardinal sin,
When he'd dug them all up in the past.
He meant not to fight with the cat from next door;
But he's done it, the villain. He's done it.
That he'd never lift paw up in anger he swore;
But it happened; and now, he's aghast.

Uri-Uriah, we've great apprehensions.
You know what they say about good intentions?

. . . AN XTROVERT CAT

Xodus here is the cat who will greet you,
Give you a welcome on getting back home.
Xodus always looks happy to meet you,
Even on Friday, the day for his comb.

Endlessly cordial with people who're calling,
Xodus loves to jump up on their knees.
Some of them find his attentions appalling
(Often the ones who are hardest to please!)

Equally friendly to neighbouring felines,
Xodus hasn't 'had words' with one yet.
No sooner sees them than starts making beelines,
Being so very 'hail-pussy-well-met'.

Hardly surprising his social life's frantic,
Or that he's known and well thought of for miles.
Loving excursions (and some are romantic!),
He's the original cat-on-the-tiles.

Seldom indoors long, he's to-ing and fro-ing,
Paying respects to a friend or old flame.
Never was cat so completely outgoing.
That's how he came to be given his name!

. . . A YES-CAT

Yea-verily's always so wonderf'lly willing.
Just ask and he'll lap up his milk without spilling.
He'll finish a meal to the last little piece,
Together with all of the gristle and grease;
And if he has found it supremely delicious,
He's happy to give you a hand with the dishes
(A claim which, although it may seem overblown,
Is true in so far as he washes his own).
He's not like so many, forever complaining
When not getting out of the house, if it's raining.
He's not like his mother, who turned tail and fled,
Whenever you wanted to put her to bed.
It's seldom he's scolded. It's seldom he needs it.
One telling's enough and Yea-verily heeds it,
As if for the whole of his life he's aspired
To give satisfaction, to do what's required;
In all things to yield, to accept, acquiesce,
Concede and consent and moreover, say 'yes'.
That's why he's no scratcher, no biter, no brawler.
The other cats find him a right little crawler!

. . . A ZESTFUL CAT

Zaccheus is here! Now Zaccheus is there!
He's never at peace for two minutes, I swear.
One moment, he's busily biffing his ball;
The next, he'll be giving his mouse a maul.

He leaps and he lunges; he'll stalk and he'll spring;
He uses the lounge as his own circus ring;
And wrestles and rolls with the tortoiseshell cat
Like any professional acrobat.

And there on the floor, as he twists and he kicks,
He constantly strives to discover new tricks.
You have to restrain him, though, after a while;
It's not very good for the Wilton pile.

The garden's much better for antics like these;
Zaccheus's passion is climbing up trees.
He does it with such a spectacular bound,
You'd think he'd been chased by an Afghan hound.

He's such a remarkably vigorous tom.
Where *does* he get all of that energy from?
I'd love you to meet him; but well, the truth is
Zaccheus is taking a well-earned ziz.

zzz!